A Generous Spirit

THE TRUE STORY OF SAINT NICHOLAS

A Generous Spirit: The True Story of Saint Nicholas
Copyright © 2016 by Gwendolyn Sullivan
Illustrations & Cover Design by Kristen Polson
www.designsunlight.com

ISBN-13: 978-1542367059
ISBN-10: 1542367050

Printed by CreateSpace, an Amazon.com Company

For Abigail & Samuel –

You are the two precious inspirations
for writing this story.
I pray that even as you embrace truth
throughout your lives,
your sense of wonder and imagination
will only grow more and more.

I love you.

I know you have heard
The stories of old
Where legends of Saint Nick
Have often been told

But where do they come from
These tales we adore
Are they stories from history
Or simply folklore

Let's travel through time
Maybe even through space
To see how he lived
And there make our case

Going far back
Before the Dark Ages
We'll there find a boy
Who had tragic changes

A.D. 270

His mother and father
Had been terribly ill
And they were called up to heaven
Leaving Nick love and goodwill

They had taught him of God
Of His love and His grace
And also of Jesus
Who died in our place

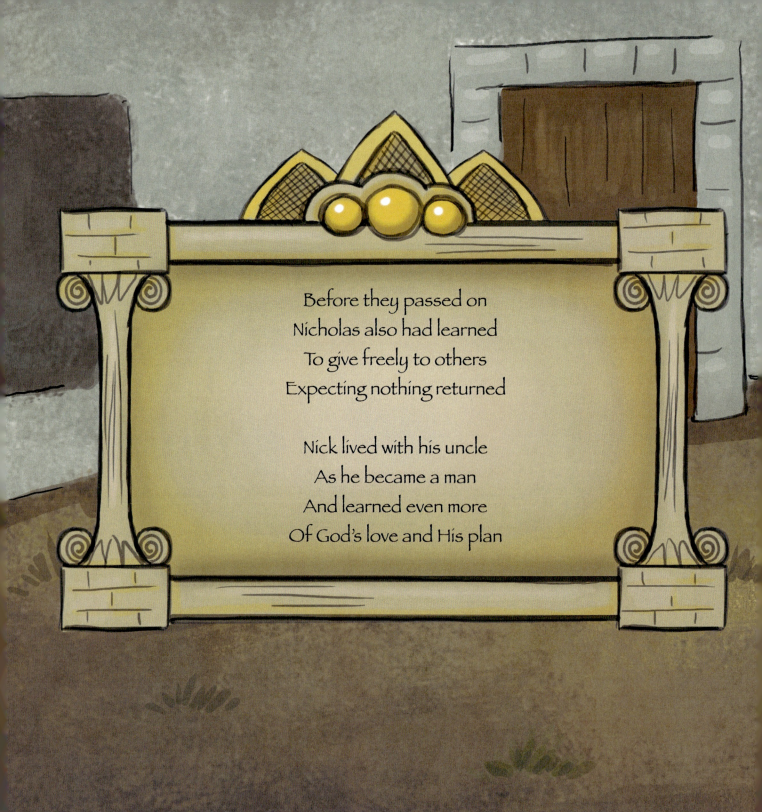

Before they passed on
Nicholas also had learned
To give freely to others
Expecting nothing returned

Nick lived with his uncle
As he became a man
And learned even more
Of God's love and His plan

He traveled to the Holy Land
To visit and retrace
The steps Jesus took
To show us His grace

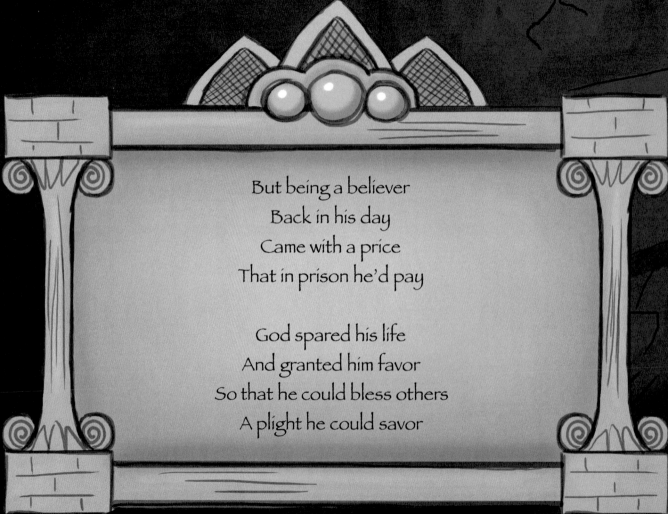

But being a believer
Back in his day
Came with a price
That in prison he'd pay

God spared his life
And granted him favor
So that he could bless others
A plight he could savor

Even so as he grew
Well, so did his heart
Using the wealth of his parents
He gave to the poor as a start

Doing it in secret
He gave to the needy
Providing for all
Without being greedy

He gave to the hungry
The poor and the weak
Dropping coins through a window
Without making a peep

He did this for years
Even to his last days
And after he died
Others continued his ways

And so, my dear friend,
As Christmas draws near
I pray you'll remember
The reason we cheer

It's not for the presents
Or the trees or the lights
Or even for Saint Nick
Whose legend shines bright

Saint Nicholas honored
All the year through
How providing for others
Was what Jesus would do

For Christmas reminds us
Of love, mercy, and grace
When God's greatest gift came
Our sins to erase

About the Author:

Gwendolyn is a wife and stay-at-home/work part-time from home mom from Oklahoma. Her hobbies before being blessed with children included writing and being involved in her local community theatre. While those things are still occasional pastimes, her current passion is to raise her children to love Jesus and to love and serve others.

About the Illustrator:

Kristen has been a graphic designer and illustrator since 2002 and more recently served as an art teacher. She and her husband own Design Sunlight, a creative solutions company that focuses on growth and community outreach. They have five beautiful children and reside in Oklahoma.

Made in the USA
Las Vegas, NV
26 November 2023